DEAR POET

NOTES TO A YOUNG WRITER

Dear Poet

Notes to a Young Writer

*A Poetic Journey into the Creative Process for
Readers, Writers, Artists, & Dreamers*

Charles Ghigna

RESOURCE *Publications* • Eugene, Oregon

DEAR POET: NOTES TO A YOUNG WRITER
A Poetic Journey into the Creative Process for Readers, Writers,
Artists, & Dreamers

Resource Publications
An Imprint of Wipf and Stock Publishers
199 W. 8th Ave., Suite 3
Eugene, OR 97401

www.wipfandstock.com

PAPERBACK ISBN: 978-1-5326-9256-7
HARDCOVER ISBN: 978-1-5326-9257-4
EBOOK ISBN: 978-1-5326-9258-1

Manufactured in the U.S.A.   AUGUST 5, 2019

for Chip Ghigna,
the heart of the poet,
the eye of the artist,
the daring of the dreamer

and for Debra,
always

"Poetry is not only dream and vision;
it is the skeleton architecture of our lives.
It lays the foundations for a future of change,
a bridge across our fears of what has never been before."

—AUDRE LORDE

Introduction

As I ENTER MY seventh decade on this planet, I wonder what words of wisdom I might have written to the younger me. What treasured tidbits have I learned along the way? What could I leave in a letter to young artists and poets searching the world for advice, guidance, and inspiration.

I began as I always do, by closing my eyes and listening to that soft voice that has spoken without fail for more than a half century. The voice spoke. I took notes. Here they are. Little poetic pieces I trust will speak to future generations of readers, writers, artists and dreamers. May you continue to listen. May you continue to speak.

I.

Do not tell

the world

your pain.

Show it

the joy

of your tears.

II.

Hang a picture

of truth

in your heart.

Let the mirror

of your eyes

fill the page.

III.

4

A simple

truth

is light.

A complex

lie

is fire.

IV.

When in need

of the poem,

go write it.

But do not think

you are

needed.

There is no

need

for the poet.

There is only

need

for the poem.

V.

Do not write

another word—

unless you have to.

VI.

No matter

how many poems

you write

to keep

yourself alive,

you cannot.

VII.

Run.

Yell.

Spit at the dark.

Curse the moon.

Throw rocks

at the stars.

Get it all out.

Get it all out.

Get it all out on paper.

VIII.

Style is not

how you

write.

It is how

you do not

write

like

anyone

else.

IX.

Trust

your instincts

to write.

Question

your reasons

not to.

X.

Inspiration,

like lightning,

comes

from the

darkest

clouds.

XI.

Look in the mirror.

If you see a stranger,

write a poem.

If you see

your father,

write a poem.

If you see

yourself,

put down the pen.

XII.

A silent rhyme

upon the page

is what the poet gives,

gentle words

whispered in trust

to see if memory lives.

XIII.

The path

to inspiration starts

upon a trail unknown.

Each writer's block

is not a rock.

It is a stepping stone.

XIV.

Poems are not penned

to the page

waiting for us to admire.

They are only

lonely thoughts

caught by tears on fire.

XV.

Don't plant

your poem

on the page

as though

you're hanging

drapes.

Its shape

and flow

should come

and grow

like wild

summer grapes.

XVI.

A poet's life

is paradox.

It's more than what it seems.

We write

of our reality.

The one inside our dreams.

XVII.

A poem

is the echo of a promise,

the thunder of a sigh,

the music

of a memory,

a child asking why.

XVIII.

A poem

is a rising moon

shining on the sea,

an afterglow

of all you know,

of all your dreams set free.

XIX.

A poem

is a spider web

spun with words of wonder,

woven lace

held in place

by whispers made of thunder.

X X.

A poem

is a firefly

upon the summer wind.

Instead of shining

where she goes,

she lights up where she's been.

XXI.

It's not the poem

on the page

that makes them laugh or cry.

It's how your soul

touched a heart

and opened up an eye.

XXII.

A poem
is a play
meant to delight you.

A poem
is a party
meant to excite you.

A poem
is a song
full of desire.

A poem
is a sunset
meant to inspire.

A poem
is a secret
shared among friends.

A poem
is a promise
that never ends.

XXIII.

A poem

is a whisper, a shout,

thoughts turned inside out.

A poem

is a laugh, a sigh,

an echo passing by.

A poem

is a rhythm, a rhyme,

a moment caught in time.

A poem

is a moon, a star,

a glimpse of who you are.

XXIV.

The answer

to the artist

comes quicker than a blink,

though the spark

of inspiration

is not what you might think.

The muse

is full of magic,

though her vision may be dim.

The artist

does not choose the work.

It is the work that chooses him.